Message from the Secretary

January 19, 2016

I hereby present the following "Entry/Exit Overstay Report" prepared by the Department of Homeland Security (DHS). Pursuant to the requirement contained in Division F, Title I of P.L. 114-113, the Consolidated Appropriations Act, 2016, and 8 U.S.C. 1376, DHS is submitting this report on overstay data.

DHS has generated this report to provide data on departures and overstays, by country, for foreign visitors to the United States who were expected to depart in Fiscal Year (FY) 2015 (October 1, 2014-September 30, 2015).

This report is being provided to the following Members of Congress:

The Honorable Harold Rogers
Chairman, House Committee on Appropriations

The Honorable Nita M. Lowey
Ranking Member, House Committee on Appropriations

The Honorable Bob Goodlatte
Chairman, House Committee on the Judiciary

The Honorable John Conyers, Jr.
Ranking Member, House Committee on the Judiciary

The Honorable Michael McCaul
Chairman, House Committee on Homeland Security

The Honorable Bennie Thompson
Ranking Member, House Committee on Homeland Security

The Honorable Thad Cochran
Chairman, Senate Committee on Appropriations

The Honorable Barbara Mikulski
Vice Chairwoman, Senate Committee on Appropriations

The Honorable Charles Grassley
Chairman, Senate Committee on the Judiciary

The Honorable Patrick Leahy
Ranking Member, Senate Committee on the Judiciary

The Honorable Ron Johnson
Chairman, Senate Committee on Homeland Security and Governmental Affairs

The Honorable Thomas R. Carper
Ranking Member, Senate Committee on Homeland Security and Governmental Affairs

Inquiries relating to this report may be directed to the DHS Office of Legislative Affairs at (202) 447-5890.

Sincerely,

Jeh Charles Johnson

Executive Summary

Pursuant to the requirement contained in Division F, Title I of P.L. 114-113, the Consolidated Appropriations Act, 2016, and 8 U.S.C. 1376, the Department of Homeland Security is submitting this report on overstay data. This report is submitted to provide data on departures and overstays, by country, for foreign visitors who were admitted to the United States though air and sea Ports of Entry (POEs), and who were expected to depart in FY 2015 (October 1, 2014-September 30, 2015).

An overstay is a nonimmigrant who was lawfully admitted to the United States for an authorized period but stayed or remains in the United States beyond his or her lawful admission period. DHS identifies two types of overstays—those individuals for whom no departure has been recorded (Suspected In-Country Overstay) and those individuals whose departure was recorded after their lawful admission period expired (Out-of-Country Overstay). The overstay identification process is conducted through arrival, departure and immigration status information, consolidated to generate a complete picture of individuals traveling to the United States as described below.

U.S. Customs and Border Protection (CBP) receives passenger manifest data on all commercial and private air and commercial sea arrivals to and departures from the United States. These manifests indicate who is onboard the aircraft or vessel. In the land environment, CBP receives traveler data on third country nationals departing to Canada. Additionally, CBP is able to reconcile a significant portion of travelers who arrive through our borders with both Canada and Mexico as the majority of those travelers are frequent crossers and CBP is able to close a previous arrival when a new arrival is recorded.

Upon arrival in the United States, CBP officers interview every traveler to determine the purpose and intent of travel. CBP officers also confirm the accuracy of the biographic manifest data provided by the carriers, who are subject to fines for any missing or inaccurate data. For most foreign nationals, the person's fingerprint biometrics and digital photograph are collected.

For departing travelers, air and sea carriers provide biographic manifest data for all travelers prior to leaving the United States. The carriers are required by law to provide specific sets of data, which include name and passport number, and they are subject to fines for missing or inaccurate data. The biographic departure data are then matched against arrival data to determine who has complied with the terms of admission and who has overstayed. CBP maintains a separate system specifically for this purpose. This system also receives other DHS data relevant to whether a person is lawfully present-such as immigration benefit information or information on student visitors to the United States.

It is very important to point out that determining lawful status is more complicated than simply matching entry and exit data. For example, a person may receive a six month stay at the time of entry but then apply for and receive an extension of that six months while in the United States—which is relevant in determining if a person is truly an overstay or not.

Arrivals to and departures from the United States are by definition fluid, and for the purposes of a written report, "cutoff dates" were established. Unless otherwise noted, for the charts embedded within this report, the totals refer to departures that were expected to take place between October 1, 2014 and September 30, 2015.

This report is limited to foreign nationals who entered the United States as nonimmigrant visitors for business (i.e., B-1 and WB visas) or pleasure (i.e., B-2 and WT visas) through an air or sea POE. DHS has determined that there were a total of 44,928,381 nonimmigrant admissions to the United States for business or pleasure through air or sea POEs that were expected to depart in FY 2015, which represents the vast majority of annual nonimmigrant admissions. Of this number, DHS calculated a total overstay rate of 1.17 percent, or 527,127 individuals. In other words, 98.83 percent had left the United States on time and abided by the terms of their admission.

This report breaks the overstay rates down further to provide a better picture of those overstays that remain in the United States beyond their period of admission and for whom no evidence of a departure or transition to another immigration status. At the end of FY 2015, there were 482,781 Suspected In-Country Overstays. The overall Suspected In-Country Overstay rate for this scope of travelers is 1.07 percent of the expected departures.

Due to continuing departures by individuals in this population, by January 4, 2016, the number of Suspected In-Country Overstays for FY 2015 had dropped to 416,500, rendering the Suspected In-Country Overstay rate as 0.9 percent. In other words, as of January 4, 2016, DHS has been able to confirm the departures of more than 99 percent of nonimmigrant visitors scheduled to depart in FY 2015 via air and sea POEs, and that number continues to grow.

This report separates Visa Waiver Program (VWP) country overstay numbers from non-VWP country numbers. For VWP countries, the FY 2015 Suspected In-Country Overstay rate is 0.65 percent of the 20,974,390 expected departures. For non-VWP countries, the FY 2015 Suspected In-Country Overstay rate is 1.60 percent of the 13,182,807 expected departures. DHS is in the process of evaluating whether and to what extent the data presented in this report will be used to make decisions on the VWP country designations.

For Canada and Mexico the FY 2015 Suspected In-Country Overstay rate is 1.18 percent of the 7,875,054 expected departures and 1.45 percent of the 2,896,130 expected departures respectively. Consistent with the methodology for other countries, this represents only travel through air and sea ports of entry and does not include data on land border crossings.

Entry/Exit Overstay Report

Table of Contents

I. Background

The purpose of this report is to identify country-by-country overstay rates for certain classes of admission.

U.S. Customs and Border Protection (CBP) collects biographic information on all nonimmigrant arrivals to the United States through an inspection by a CBP officer. In the air and sea environment, CBP officers validate the manifest information provided by commercial and private aircraft operators. For many nonimmigrants, submission of biometric information is also required upon admission and is captured in the presence of a CBP officer.[1] In addition, CBP has strengthened the document requirements at air, land, and sea Ports of Entry (POEs) by reducing the number of accepted travel documents one may use to enter the United States,[2] which in turn has increased CBP's ability to quickly and accurately collect information on arriving aliens, particularly at the land borders.

The United States did not build its border, aviation, and immigration infrastructure with exit processing in mind. Consequently, United States airports do not have designated areas exclusively for travelers leaving the United States. Instead, departures of travelers are recorded biographically using outbound passenger manifests provided by commercial carriers. Under regulations governing the Advance Passenger Information System, carriers are required to validate the manifest information against the travel document being presented before a traveler is permitted to board their aircraft or sea vessel.

In the land environment, travelers arrive at land POEs via various modes of transportation, including cars, trains, buses, ferries, bicycles, trucks, and on foot. There are major physical infrastructure, logistical, and operational hurdles to collect an individual's biographic and biometric data upon departure. Due to the existing limitations in collecting departure data in the land environment, this report does not include departure and overstay information from those travelers who entered the United States through a land POE. CBP is addressing these limitations through various efforts, including increased information sharing and partnerships, targeted operations, analyzing land POE departure traffic, and several pilots to experiment with innovative means of collecting biometric information from individuals departing via land POEs.

The Department of Homeland Security (DHS) anticipates the ability to provide a broader scope of data in future Entry/Exit Overstay Reports. Efforts by CBP, as described in this report, are ongoing and will continue to improve the existing process and availability of departure data.

---

[1] 8 C.F.R. § 235.1(f)(1)(ii)

[2] The Western Hemisphere Travel Initiative is a joint U.S. State Department/DHS initiative that implemented § 7209 of the Intelligence Reform and Terrorism Prevention Act of 2004 (Pub. L. No. 108-458), which limited the documents that could be used to enter the United States.

II. Existing Operations

Congress transitioned entry/exit policy and operations to CBP through the *Fiscal Year (FY) 2013 DHS Appropriations Act* (Pub. L. No. 113-6) in order to centralize the entry/exit mission in one place within DHS. The entry/exit mission is to successfully capture and match the arrival and departure records of foreign nationals who visit the United States in order to help determine who is lawfully abiding by, or violating, immigration law. Capture of departure information also contributes significantly to CBP security-related missions, such as counterterrorism or other law enforcement functions.

A. Air and Sea Environments

Today, in the air/sea environments, CBP obtains entry records through both carrier-provided manifest data and inspections conducted by CBP officers. CBP obtains biographic data on travelers who lawfully enter or depart the United States by air or sea.[3] Air and sea carriers are required by law to submit passenger manifests to CBP, which are then recorded as arrivals or departures from the United States.[4] Air carriers are required to provide data not simply on who has made a reservation for a particular flight, but who is actually on the aircraft at the time the aircraft departs.[5] Airlines are subject to fines for making errors regarding who is or is not on any particular aircraft.[6]

Although CBP currently obtains biographic arrival and departure information on almost all foreign nationals in the air/sea environment, and biometric entry data in the air environment, CBP plans to improve the existing process in the future, as follows:

- Biometric Exit Mobile: During the summer of 2015, CBP began collecting a sample of biometric exit data using mobile fingerprint collection devices on selected flights departing from major air POEs. This has afforded a small amount of biometric departure data and provided a significant law enforcement benefit for existing outbound operations. The current airports using this technology are: Chicago/O'Hare (ORD); Atlanta/Hartsfield (ATL); New York (JFK); Newark (EWR); Los Angeles (LAX); San Francisco (SFO); Miami (MIA); Dallas/Ft. Worth (DFW); Washington/Dulles (IAD); and Houston/George Bush (IAH). The goals of the program are to: 1) determine the percentage of reconciled departures that without biometrics would have gone unresolved; 2) identify enforcement needs for a comprehensive biometric exit solution across all air ports of entry; and, 3) validate carrier provided manifest information.

---

[3] In addition, the Department obtains biometric information on all nonimmigrants who enter the United States via air and sea, except for those who are exempt by regulation, which includes those over the age of 79 or under 14, diplomats, and certain other discrete categories. See 8 C.F.R. § 215.1(f)(1)(ii).
[4] 8 C.F.R. § 231.1, see also 70 Fed. Reg. 17849 (Apr. 7, 2005) (describing the specific data elements for each passenger that carriers are required to provide).
[5] 19 C.F.R. §§ 122.49(a); 122.74(a).
[6] 8 U.S.C. § 1221(g).

- Biometric Exit Field Trial: In late 2016, CBP will deploy a biometric exit field trial, which will test new technologies in collecting biometric data from departing air environment foreign nationals. This will be a comprehensive pilot that incorporates additional biometric modalities and is designed to inform a future nationwide deployment.

- New Reporting Environment: The *FY 2015 DHS Appropriations Act* provided $9.9 million for a new reporting environment for the Arrival and Departure Information System, which will allow CBP to track entry/exit and overstay data on a monthly or weekly basis, as needed. These funds are being used to build the new reporting environment during 2016.

B. Land Environment

The collection of departure information in the land environment is more difficult than in the air/sea environment due to the lack of electronically captured and provided information of who is exiting the United States. In the land environment, there is no such requirement for advance reporting of arrivals and departures, as the majority of travelers cross the borders using their own vehicle or as a pedestrian.

1.   Northern Border

On the Northern border, CBP is addressing this limitation through a partnership with the Canada Border Services Agency. The Beyond the Border agreement[7] provides for an entry/exit initiative that has been implemented, under which Canada and the United States have agreed to exchange entry records for land crossings between the two countries, so that an entry into one is recorded as an exit from the other.

On June 30, 2013, Canada and the United States began exchanging entry data for third-country nationals, permanent residents of Canada, and U.S. lawful permanent residents, who enter through land POEs along the shared border, where information is collected electronically. As a result of this initiative, the United States now has a working land border exit system on its Northern border for non-U.S. and non-Canadian citizens. CBP is currently matching 99.13 percent of the entry information received from Canada to an entry in the Arrival Departure Information System.

Both countries plan to expand the program to include all travelers in the future.

---

[7] United States-Canada Beyond the Border: A Shared Vision for Perimeter Security and Economic Competitiveness, Action Plan, Dec. 2011. Accessible at http://www.whitehouse.gov/sites/default/files/us-canada_btb_action_plan3.pdf.

2. Southern Border

The Southwest border with Mexico does not provide the same opportunities as the Northern border with Canada, because Mexico's infrastructure and data collection capabilities at the shared U.S.-Mexico border are currently more limited. As a result, CBP is exploring the best methods of obtaining data from travelers departing the United States and entering Mexico by land, including:

- "Pulse and surge" operations:[8] These operations are ongoing and provide some outbound departure information on travelers departing the United States and entering Mexico.

- Land Exit Pilot: In early 2016, CBP deployed a pilot at the Otay Mesa POE in California that collects biographic data from all departing travelers and biometric information from departing foreign national travelers in the pedestrian environment. The Otay Mesa pilot will help CBP identify future technologies and processes that could be used for cost-effective biographic and biometric exit data collection at land POEs.

- Southern Border traffic analysis: CBP has also completed a study analyzing the traffic patterns and reentry of travelers who enter the United States through the southwest land border. CBP plans to use it to determine the optimal places for CBP to place its existing resources in order to best collect departure information and target overstays.

To account for limited information available on foreign nationals departing into Mexico through the southwest border, CBP employs several measures: ongoing Pulse and Surge operations provide some outbound departure information on travelers departing the United States and entering Mexico; land I-94 forms (forms provided upon entry that are to be returned upon departure) voluntarily turned in at the borders by foreign nationals leaving the country are collected and recorded; and subjects who enter the United States and subsequently return to the United States without an identified exit are reconciled for the prior trip due to subsequent entry.

C. Overstay Definition

An overstay is a nonimmigrant who was lawfully admitted to the United States for an authorized period but stayed in the United States beyond his or her lawful admission period. This also includes a nonimmigrant admitted for "duration of status" who fails to maintain that status. "Duration of status" is a term used for foreign nationals who are admitted for a specific purpose, which expires when that purpose expires—such as a student program that runs for four years of study.

---

[8] "Pulse and Surge" operations are strategies whereby CBP officers monitor outbound traffic on the U.S. southern border. See Testimony of Commissioner Alan Bersin, Commissioner of U.S. Customs and Border Protection, before the Senate Caucus on International Narcotics Control, Mar. 9, 2011. Accessible at http://www.dhs.gov/news/2011/03/09/testimony-commissioner-alan-bersin-us-customs-and-border-protection-senate-caucus. Although the purpose of "pulse and surge" is to counter traffic in drugs, currency, and firearms into Mexico, data collected during these operations can be used to create departure records for foreign nationals.

The Department classifies individuals as overstays by matching departure and status change records to arrival records collected during the admission process. The Department identifies individuals as having overstayed if their departure record shows they departed the United States after their lawful admission period expired.[9] (i.e., Out-of-Country Overstays). While these individuals are considered overstays, there is evidence indicating they are no longer physically present in the United States. DHS also identifies individuals as possible overstays if there are no records of a departure or change in status[10] prior to the end of their authorized admission period (i.e., Suspected In-Country Overstays).

In this report, the Department presents ADIS system-generated overstay rates by country of citizenship for nonimmigrant visitors for business or pleasure[11] who were admitted to the United States through an air or sea[12] POE, regardless of overstay type. These classes of admission made up 85 percent of the total number of visits by nonimmigrants who arrived by air or sea and who were expected to depart in FY 2015. While significant progress has been made, challenges remain with integration of systems used in the travel continuum for reporting on visa categories beyond business or pleasure. In light of these and other data limitations, DHS is in the process of evaluating whether and to what extent the data presented in this report will be used to make decisions on VWP country designations. Enhancements are currently underway focusing on the remaining visa categories, most notably starting with student visitor classes (F, M and J visas). Subsequent annual Entry/Exit Overstay Reports expect to include additional classes of visitors to the United States as integration of these systems progress.

---

[9] In these cases, DHS sanctions the individual who overstayed their authorized period of stay in the U.S. according to existing immigration law, which is based on a sliding scale of penalties depending on the length of time unlawfully present in the United States. See, e.g., 8 U.S.C. § 1202(g) (nonimmigrant visa is voided at conclusion of authorized period of stay, if an individual remains in the United States beyond the authorized period); 8 U.S.C. § 1187(a)(7) (referring to VWP, "if the alien previously was admitted without a visa under this section, the alien must not have failed to comply with the conditions of any previous admission as such a nonimmigrant"); and 8 U.S.C. § 1182(a)(9)(B)(i)(I) and (II) (alien inadmissible for 3 years if unlawfully present for more than 180 days but less than a year; alien inadmissible for 10 years if unlawfully present for a year or more, pursuant to various provisions of the Immigration and Nationality Act).

[10] Pending immigration benefit applications and approved extensions of stay, change of nonimmigrant status, or adjustment of status to lawful permanent residence may extend the authorized period of stay. For example, upon entering the United States a person may be granted a six-month period of admission, but thereafter lawfully change immigration status prior to the expiration of that period, and in turn be authorized to stay beyond the initial six months. Generally, these options are not available to those who enter under VWP. 8 C.F.R. § 245.1(a)(8); 8 C.F.R. § 248.2(a)(6).

[11] Visitors for business or pleasure include the following classes of admission: visitor for business (B-1), visitor for pleasure (B-2), visa waiver visitor for business (WB), and visa waiver visitor for pleasure (WT).

[12] The sea overstay rates are only reflective of the population that initially entered the United States through a sea POE but is not reflective of all traveler arrivals where the vessel both departs from and subsequently arrives at the same location (commonly referred to as "closed loop" cruises.) For example, if a foreign national already within the United States departs from the Port Canaveral, Florida Seaport for a seven day cruise in the Caribbean and subsequently re-enters at Port Canaveral, then that arrival would not be taken into account for the purposes of this report.

D. Overstay Identification and Action

CBP maintains arrival/departure information for all foreign nationals based on border crossings and carrier data. This information is used to generate daily overstay lists. These system-generated overstay lists are sent for checks against the CBP Automated Targeting System (ATS) and the U.S. Citizenship and Immigration Services CLAIMS3 database, reducing the overall list size by providing additional checks and identifying persons who have departed the United States or changed into another nonimmigrant or immigrant status. The ATS then applies screening rules, as defined by U.S. Immigration and Customs Enforcement (ICE), to prioritize system-identified overstays. This creates a prioritized overstay list which is sent to ICE.

The Homeland Security Investigations (HSI) Counterterrorism and Criminal Exploitation Unit (CTCEU) at ICE is dedicated to the enforcement of nonimmigrant visa violations. Each year, CTCEU analyzes records of hundreds of thousands of potential status violators from various investigative databases and DHS entry/exit registration systems. To better manage investigative resources, CTCEU relies on a prioritization framework for these leads established in consultation with interagency partners within the national intelligence and federal law enforcement communities. Those identified as posing a potential national security threat to the United States are prioritized and referred to ICE HSI field offices for investigation. Leads that do not meet national security criteria for ICE HSI are referred to ICE's Enforcement and Removal Operations.

HSI Special Agents and analysts continuously monitor threat reports and proactively address emergent issues. This practice has contributed to ICE's counterterrorism mission by initiating or supporting high-priority national security initiatives based upon specific intelligence. The goal is to identify, locate, prosecute where applicable, and remove those overstays posing real or potential national security threats to the United States. This is accomplished through both broad intelligence-driven criteria on subjects that exhibit similar characteristics of known radical organizations and their participants and by activity which focuses ICE investigations on those subjects that are considered to pose a higher risk to national security.

Pursuant to DHS immigration enforcement priorities, ICE Enforcement and Removal Operations (ERO) will review and take appropriate enforcement action derived from information gained from the DHS data. Additionally, ERO also encounters overstays who meet a DHS priority via its enforcement programs such as Fugitive Operations and the Criminal Alien Program.

In January 2012, CTCEU initiated the use of the National Counterterrorism Center (NCTC) in support of its Overstay Program to screen overstays by identifying potential matches to derogatory intelligence community holdings.

III. Overstay Rates

Tables 1 and 2 below present the overstay rates for countries that participate in the Visa Waiver Program (VWP) (Table 1) and countries that do not (Table 2). Table 3 includes nationals of Canada and Mexico only. It is important to note that the total number of FY 2015 overstays, as identified in this report, does not equal the total number of FY 2015 overstays that currently remain in the United States. That number is likely lower. This is because foreign nationals identified as possible overstays can and do subsequently depart the United States, or have been found to have adjusted their lawful status. For purposes of this report, these are still considered overstays.

For all charts, "Expected Departures" is the number of travelers from each country that were admitted to the United States as a nonimmigrant and whose expected departure date occurred within FY 2015. "Out-of-Country Overstays" refers to cases in which the Department received a departure record for a traveler, and the record indicated that the traveler departed after the authorized period of admission expired. "Suspected In-Country Overstays" refers to cases in which DHS has no departure record, or any other encounter indicating the traveler departed in FY 2015, and no evidence that the person transitioned into a lawful immigration status. The "Overstay Rate" is the percentage of travelers from each country who overstayed their period of admission to the United States, regardless of type.[13]

These charts represent data from FY 2015 only. The Department determined that there were a total of 44,928,381 nonimmigrant admissions to the United States for business or pleasure through air or sea POEs that were expected to depart in FY 2015. Of this number, the Department calculated a total overstay rate of 1.17 percent, or 527,127 individuals. In other words, 98.83 percent had left the United States on time and abided by the terms of their admission.

At the end of FY 2015, Suspected In-Country Overstays were 482,781 individuals, with a Suspected In-Country Overstay rate of 1.07 percent. This data indicates that 98.93 percent had departed the United States or transitioned to a lawful immigration status.

Upon finalizing this report, DHS identified approximately 66,500 travelers who are listed in this report as Suspected In-Country Overstays, but have subsequently departed the United States as of January 4, 2016. Therefore, as of January 4, 2016, the Department identified approximately 416,500 Suspected In-Country Overstays or a revised FY 2015 Suspected In-Country Overstay rate of 0.9 percent. In other words, as of January 4, 2016, DHS has been able to confirm the

---

[13] Rates are shown for countries as well as passport-issuing authorities and places of origin recognized by the United States. With respect to all references to "country" or "countries" in this document, section 4(b)(1) of the Taiwan Relations Act of 1979 (Pub. L. No. 96-8), provides that "[w]henever the laws of the United States refer or relate to foreign countries, nations, states, governments, or similar entities, such terms shall include and such laws shall apply with respect to Taiwan." 22 U.S.C. § 3303(b)(1). Accordingly, references to "country" or "countries" in the VWP authorizing legislation, section 217 of the Immigration and Nationality Act (8 U.S.C. § 1187), are read to include Taiwan. This is consistent with the United States' one-China policy, under which the United States has maintained unofficial relations with Taiwan since 1979. Taiwan entered the VWP on October 2, 2012.

departures of more than 99 percent of nonimmigrant visitors scheduled to depart in FY 2015 via air and sea POEs, and that number continues to grow.

For VWP countries, the FY 2015 Suspected In-Country Overstay rate is 0.65 percent of the 20,974,390 expected departures. For non-VWP countries, the FY 2015 Suspected In-Country Overstay rate is 1.60 percent of the 13,182,807 expected departures.

For Canada and Mexico the FY 2015 Suspected In-Country Overstay rate is 1.18 percent of the 7,875,054 expected departures and 1.45 percent of the 2,896,130 expected departures respectively.

Table 1
FY 2015 Overstay rates for nonimmigrant visitors admitted to the United States for business or pleasure (WB/WT/B-1/B-2) via air and sea POEs for VWP Countries[14],[15]

Country of Citizenship	Expected Departures	Out-of-Country Overstays	Suspected In-Country Overstays	Total Overstays	Total Overstay Rate	Suspected In-Country Overstay Rate
Andorra	1,221	2	3	5	0.41%	0.24%
Australia	1,306,352	878	3,964	4,842	0.37%	0.30%
Austria	210,854	119	2,694	2,813	1.33%	1.28%
Belgium	290,103	158	1,477	1,635	0.56%	0.51%
Brunei	1,143	1	10	11	0.96%	0.87%
Chile	306,598	584	6,553	7,137	2.33%	2.14%
Czech Republic	97,708	186	1,422	1,608	1.65%	1.46%
Denmark	326,334	158	1,812	1,970	0.60%	0.56%
Estonia	20,247	43	191	234	1.16%	0.94%
Finland	153,136	91	747	838	0.55%	0.49%
France	1,767,377	1,434	11,973	13,407	0.76%	0.68%
Germany	2,107,035	1,160	21,394	22,554	1.07%	1.02%
Greece	71,430	320	1,333	1,653	2.31%	1.87%
Hungary	75,904	356	1,860	2,216	2.92%	2.45%
Iceland	51,231	36	199	235	0.46%	0.39%
Ireland	453,597	316	1,797	2,113	0.47%	0.40%

[14] Effective January 12, 2009, citizens or nationals from VWP countries are required to obtain an approved travel authorization via ESTA to be eligible to travel to the United States by air or sea under the VWP. Upon admission into the United States, visitors are classified either under a WT (waiver-tourist) or a WB (waiver-business) status.
[15] Citizens or nationals of VWP countries may also obtain and travel to the United States on a B-1/B-2 visa and seek admission under the B-1 or B-2 nonimmigrant classification.

Table 1

FY 2015 Overstay rates for nonimmigrant visitors admitted to the United States for business or pleasure (WB/WT/B-1/B-2) via air and sea POEs for VWP Countries[14,15]

Country of Citizenship	Expected Departures	Out-of-Country Overstays	Suspected In-Country Overstays	Total Overstays	Total Overstay Rate	Suspected In-Country Overstay Rate
Italy	1,184,715	1,336	17,661	18,997	1.60%	1.49%
Japan	3,014,769	455	5,603	6,058	0.20%	0.19%
Korea, South	1,121,890	1,352	7,120	8,472	0.76%	0.63%
Latvia	18,698	86	273	359	1.92%	1.46%
Liechtenstein	2,048	2	12	14	0.68%	0.59%
Lithuania	26,502	102	480	582	2.20%	1.81%
Luxembourg	14,279	7	75	82	0.57%	0.53%
Malta	5,504	3	44	47	0.85%	0.80%
Monaco	1,136	1	4	5	0.44%	0.35%
Netherlands	709,633	461	7,723	8,184	1.15%	1.09%
New Zealand	298,093	245	1,206	1,451	0.49%	0.40%
Norway	312,600	193	1,230	1,423	0.46%	0.39%
Portugal	165,533	500	3,322	3,822	2.31%	2.01%
San Marino	702	0	16	16	2.28%	2.28%
Singapore	127,804	106	375	481	0.38%	0.29%
Slovakia	44,274	116	927	1,043	2.36%	2.09%
Slovenia	23,669	43	235	278	1.17%	0.99%
Spain	896,833	1,668	10,891	12,559	1.40%	1.21%
Sweden	576,422	354	2,428	2,782	0.48%	0.42%
Switzerland	438,910	279	2,123	2,402	0.55%	0.48%
Taiwan	356,225	704	1,184	1,888	0.53%	0.33%
United Kingdom	4,393,881	2,504	16,446	18,950	0.43%	0.37%
TOTAL	**20,974,390**	**16,359**	**136,807**	**153,166**	**0.73%**	**0.65%**

Table 2

FY 2015 Overstay rates for nonimmigrants with B-1/B-2 visas admitted to the United States for business or pleasure via air and sea POEs for non-VWP Countries (excluding Canada and Mexico)

Country Of Citizenship	Expected Departures	Out–of–Country Overstays	Suspected In-Country Overstays	Total Overstays	Total Overstay Rate	Suspected In-Country Overstay Rate
Afghanistan	2,136	13	219	232	10.86%	10.25%
Albania	6,123	24	183	207	3.38%	2.99%
Algeria	9,353	53	240	293	3.13%	2.57%
Angola	10,987	25	268	293	2.67%	2.44%
Antigua and Barbuda	13,485	29	204	233	1.73%	1.51%
Argentina	690,275	237	7,498	7,735	1.12%	1.09%
Armenia	5,962	11	195	206	3.46%	3.27%
Azerbaijan	5,758	8	72	80	1.39%	1.25%
Bahamas, The	220,305	232	1,510	1,742	0.79%	0.69%
Bahrain	7,003	12	68	80	1.14%	0.97%
Bangladesh	28,888	96	1,147	1,243	4.30%	3.97%
Barbados	53,643	57	310	367	0.68%	0.58%
Belarus	11,996	21	229	250	2.08%	1.91%
Belize	24,029	43	531	574	2.39%	2.21%
Benin	2,016	16	129	145	7.19%	6.40%
Bhutan	442	4	106	110	24.89%	23.98%
Bolivia	52,795	54	1,118	1,172	2.22%	2.12%
Bosnia and Herzegovina	6,762	21	146	167	2.47%	2.16%
Botswana	1,832	2	16	18	0.98%	0.87%
Brazil	2,350,140	1,284	35,707	36,991	1.57%	1.52%
Bulgaria	26,311	69	389	458	1.74%	1.48%
Burkina Faso	3,765	24	654	678	18.01%	17.37%
Burma	4,057	15	114	129	3.18%	2.81%
Burundi	863	2	81	83	9.62%	9.39%
Cabo Verde	4,295	10	276	286	6.66%	6.43%
Cambodia	2,497	9	46	55	2.20%	1.84%
Cameroon	7,779	77	607	684	8.79%	7.80%
Central African Republic	160	0	11	11	6.88%	6.88%
Chad	677	14	104	118	17.43%	15.36%
China	1,763,669	2,554	15,692	18,246	1.04%	0.89%
Colombia	935,500	721	16,434	17,155	1.83%	1.76%

Table 2

FY 2015 Overstay rates for nonimmigrants with B-1/B-2 visas admitted to the United States for business or pleasure via air and sea POEs for non-VWP Countries (excluding Canada and Mexico)

Country Of Citizenship	Expected Departures	Out–of-Country Overstays	Suspected In-Country Overstays	Total Overstays	Total Overstay Rate	Suspected In-Country Overstay Rate
Comoros	135	0	3	3	2.22%	2.22%
Congo (Brazzaville)	1,323	5	86	91	6.88%	6.50%
Congo (Kinshasa)	5,003	23	427	450	9.00%	8.53%
Costa Rica	224,101	123	1,986	2,109	0.94%	0.89%
Croatia	20,781	32	194	226	1.09%	0.93%
Cuba	46,826	170	895	1,065	2.27%	1.91%
Cyprus	8,357	19	94	113	1.35%	1.12%
Côte d'Ivoire	5,337	35	216	251	4.70%	4.05%
Djibouti	347	3	93	96	27.67%	26.80%
Dominica	6,830	11	258	269	3.94%	3.78%
Dominican Republic	303,095	316	6,990	7,306	2.41%	2.31%
Ecuador	348,064	260	5,612	5,872	1.69%	1.61%
Egypt	74,705	175	1,245	1,420	1.90%	1.67%
El Salvador	137,535	166	3,118	3,284	2.39%	2.27%
Equatorial Guinea	1,212	11	39	50	4.13%	3.22%
Eritrea	2,339	69	382	451	19.28%	16.33%
Ethiopia	14,296	122	492	614	4.30%	3.44%
Fiji	7,361	26	142	168	2.28%	1.93%
Gabon	1,862	12	108	120	6.45%	5.80%
Gambia, The	1,795	20	181	201	11.20%	10.08%
Georgia	6,561	13	803	816	12.44%	12.24%
Ghana	21,846	106	894	1,000	4.58%	4.09%
Grenada	9,109	26	236	262	2.88%	2.59%
Guatemala	236,043	296	5,419	5,715	2.42%	2.30%
Guinea	2,200	19	175	194	8.82%	7.95%
Guinea-Bissau	133	0	6	6	4.51%	4.51%
Guyana	41,747	63	920	983	2.36%	2.20%
Haiti	121,581	559	3,312	3,871	3.18%	2.72%
Holy See	22	0	0	0	0.00%	0.00%
Honduras	161,467	204	4,075	4,279	2.65%	2.52%
India	881,974	1,463	12,885	14,348	1.63%	1.46%
Indonesia	84,103	94	922	1,016	1.21%	1.10%

Table 2
FY 2015 Overstay rates for nonimmigrants with B-1/B-2 visas admitted to the United States for business or pleasure via air and sea POEs for non-VWP Countries (excluding Canada and Mexico)

Country Of Citizenship	Expected Departures	Out–of–Country Overstays	Suspected In-Country Overstays	Total Overstays	Total Overstay Rate	Suspected In-Country Overstay Rate
Iran	24,997	122	564	686	2.74%	2.26%
Iraq	11,147	93	681	774	6.94%	6.11%
Israel	352,627	346	2,375	2,721	0.77%	0.67%
Jamaica	240,126	338	6,614	6,952	2.90%	2.75%
Jordan	33,286	179	1,397	1,576	4.74%	4.20%
Kazakhstan	17,301	38	409	447	2.58%	2.36%
Kenya	18,336	87	475	562	3.07%	2.59%
Kiribati	119	1	1	2	1.68%	0.84%
Korea, North	29	0	1	1	3.45%	3.45%
Kuwait	45,762	344	913	1,257	2.75%	2.00%
Kyrgyzstan	2,128	10	148	158	7.43%	6.95%
Laos	1,513	27	252	279	18.44%	16.66%
Lebanon	39,438	76	930	1,006	2.55%	2.36%
Lesotho	286	0	6	6	2.10%	2.10%
Liberia	4,575	134	412	546	11.93%	9.01%
Libya	1,245	13	56	69	5.54%	4.50%
Macedonia	6,014	24	226	250	4.16%	3.76%
Madagascar	872	1	7	8	0.92%	0.80%
Malawi	1,685	6	74	80	4.75%	4.39%
Malaysia	80,451	94	1,430	1,524	1.89%	1.78%
Maldives	243	0	1	1	0.41%	0.41%
Mali	2,801	16	154	170	6.07%	5.50%
Marshall Islands	52	1	2	3	5.77%	3.85%
Mauritania	1,371	12	173	185	13.49%	12.62%
Mauritius	3,094	4	27	31	1.00%	0.87%
Micronesia, Federated States of	25	0	4	4	16.00%	16.00%
Moldova	7,230	19	359	378	5.23%	4.97%
Mongolia	9,972	29	302	331	3.32%	3.03%
Montenegro	3,972	13	148	161	4.05%	3.73%
Morocco	24,695	66	390	456	1.85%	1.58%
Mozambique	1,849	2	36	38	2.06%	1.95%
Namibia	1,560	4	10	14	0.90%	0.64%
Nauru	23	0	0	0	0.00%	0.00%

Table 2

FY 2015 Overstay rates for nonimmigrants with B-1/B-2 visas admitted to the United States for business or pleasure via air and sea POEs for non-VWP Countries (excluding Canada and Mexico)

Country Of Citizenship	Expected Departures	Out–of–Country Overstays	Suspected In-Country Overstays	Total Overstays	Total Overstay Rate	Suspected In-Country Overstay Rate
Nepal	15,332	72	492	564	3.68%	3.21%
Nicaragua	58,759	78	1,167	1,245	2.12%	1.99%
Niger	760	7	25	32	4.21%	3.29%
Nigeria	183,907	627	6,781	7,408	4.03%	3.69%
Oman	5,067	16	41	57	1.13%	0.81%
Pakistan	71,803	180	1,435	1,615	2.25%	2.00%
Palau	55	0	2	2	3.64%	3.64%
Panama	144,320	133	773	906	0.63%	0.54%
Papua New Guinea	686	6	2	8	1.17%	0.29%
Paraguay	28,781	22	466	488	1.70%	1.62%
Peru	268,000	312	4,550	4,862	1.81%	1.70%
Philippines	226,777	436	3,265	3,701	1.63%	1.44%
Poland	171,243	204	2,345	2,549	1.49%	1.37%
Qatar	13,909	68	108	176	1.27%	0.78%
Romania	63,850	165	1,153	1,318	2.06%	1.81%
Russia	289,059	239	2,705	2,944	1.02%	0.94%
Rwanda	2,652	18	92	110	4.15%	3.47%
Saint Kitts and Nevis	11,387	17	237	254	2.23%	2.08%
Saint Lucia	14,100	33	363	396	2.81%	2.57%
Saint Vincent and the Grenadines	9,097	29	335	364	4.00%	3.68%
Samoa	1,856	15	110	125	6.74%	5.93%
Sao Tome and Principe	36	0	0	0	0.00%	0.00%
Saudi Arabia	139,483	544	965	1,509	1.08%	0.69%
Senegal	7,786	23	269	292	3.75%	3.45%
Serbia	20,149	40	336	376	1.87%	1.67%
Seychelles	275	1	2	3	1.09%	0.73%
Sierra Leone	2,824	63	86	149	5.28%	3.05%
Solomon Islands	140	0	0	0	0.00%	0.00%
Somalia	144	2	2	4	2.78%	1.39%
South Africa	120,220	139	974	1,113	0.93%	0.81%

Table 2

FY 2015 Overstay rates for nonimmigrants with B-1/B-2 visas admitted to the United States for business or pleasure via air and sea POEs for non-VWP Countries (excluding Canada and Mexico)

Country Of Citizenship	Expected Departures	Out–of–Country Overstays	Suspected In-Country Overstays	Total Overstays	Total Overstay Rate	Suspected In-Country Overstay Rate
South Sudan	235	4	7	11	4.68%	2.98%
Sri Lanka	16,391	34	439	473	2.89%	2.68%
Sudan	3,734	34	278	312	8.36%	7.45%
Suriname	13,111	7	93	100	0.76%	0.71%
Swaziland	626	5	12	17	2.72%	1.92%
Syria	13,430	57	440	497	3.70%	3.28%
Tajikistan	953	7	44	51	5.35%	4.62%
Tanzania	5,711	38	127	165	2.89%	2.22%
Thailand	83,482	172	1,349	1,521	1.82%	1.62%
Timor-Leste	39	0	1	1	2.56%	2.56%
Togo	1,715	15	133	148	8.63%	7.76%
Tonga	2,398	13	150	163	6.80%	6.26%
Trinidad and Tobago	170,215	107	873	980	0.58%	0.51%
Tunisia	8,436	15	135	150	1.78%	1.60%
Turkey	161,878	238	2,227	2,465	1.52%	1.38%
Turkmenistan	1,039	6	52	58	5.58%	5.00%
Tuvalu	43	0	1	1	2.33%	2.33%
Uganda	6,761	34	259	293	4.33%	3.83%
Ukraine	73,230	185	2,299	2,484	3.39%	3.14%
United Arab Emirates	30,623	204	393	597	1.95%	1.28%
Uruguay	76,856	41	1,880	1,921	2.50%	2.45%
Uzbekistan	8,008	34	502	536	6.69%	6.27%
Vanuatu	106	0	2	2	1.89%	1.89%
Venezuela	574,651	487	12,242	12,729	2.22%	2.13%
Vietnam	72,732	394	2,285	2,679	3.68%	3.14%
Yemen	3,537	28	219	247	6.98%	6.19%
Zambia	3,434	14	73	87	2.53%	2.13%
Zimbabwe	6,559	19	140	159	2.42%	2.13%
TOTAL	**13,182,807**	**17,958**	**210,825**	**228,783**	**1.74%**	**1.60%**

Table 3
FY 2015 Overstay rates for Canadian and Mexican nonimmigrants admitted to the United States for business or pleasure via air and sea POEs

Country of Citizenship	Expected Departures	Out-of-Country Overstays	Suspected In-Country Overstays	Total Overstays	Total Overstay Rate	Suspected In-Country Overstay Rate
Canada	7,875,054	6,871	93,035	99,906	1.27%	1.18%
Mexico	2,896,130	3,158	42,114	45,272	1.56%	1.45%
TOTAL	10,771,184	10,029	135,149	145,178	1.34%	1.25%

This chart represents Canadian and Mexican nonimmigrant visitors for business or pleasure admitted at air or sea POEs who were expected to depart in FY 2015. Canada and Mexico have relatively high proportions of travelers who are admitted to the United States at land POEs. Unlike all other countries, over 95 percent of travelers from Canada or Mexico enter the United States by land. As mentioned, overstay data concerning land entries will be incorporated into future iterations of this report as projects progress.

IV. Conclusion

Identifying overstays is important for national security, public safety, immigration enforcement, and immigration benefit application processing.

Over the years, the Department has significantly improved the process and data collection for the entry process—collecting data on all admissions to the United States by foreign nationals, reducing the number of documents that are usable for entry to the United States, collecting biometric data on most foreign travelers to the United States, and checking that data against criminal and terrorist watchlists. Despite the different structure of the exit process, the Department has been able to resolve many of the issues regarding the collection of departure information from foreign nationals. Further efforts, including partnerships with other governments and the private sector (e.g., airlines, airports, cruise lines, etc.), are ongoing and will continue to improve the existing process for improved data integrity.

During the past two years, DHS has made significant progress in terms of its ability to accurately report data on overstays—progress that was made possible by congressional realignment of Department resources in order to better centralize the overall mission in identifying overstays. The Department will continue to roll out additional pilot programs during FY 2016, both biometric and biographic, that will improve the ability of CBP to accurately collect and report this data. DHS looks forward to continuing to update congressional members and staffs on its progress.

V. Appendix

Fiscal Year (FY) 2014 VWP, non-VWP, Mexico and Canada Overstay Tables

The ability to accurately and reliably estimate overstay rates is dependent on the completeness and accuracy of arrival and departure records. During the generation of the FY 2014 overstay data, DHS identified significant discrepancies regarding the data received from certain air carriers, which resulted in artificially elevated overstay rates, especially for the Netherlands, Italy, and San Marino. The nature of these errors is described in more detail below. Given the serious concerns raised with respect to the accuracy and reliability of the FY 2014 data, DHS determined that a FY 2014 report should not be issued.

These data quality issues have since been resolved, and the FY 2015 Entry/Exit Overstay Report tables are an accurate depiction of country-by-country overstay numbers for these categories of travelers. The FY 2014 data included in this Appendix is provided solely to provide transparency with regard to DHS processing of overstay data.

This Appendix contains data on departures and overstays, by country, for foreign visitors to the United States who were expected to depart in FY 2014 (October 1, 2013-September 30, 2014). The data in this Appendix is presented in the same format as the data presented in the FY 2015 Entry/Exit Overstay Report (to which this Appendix is attached).

As mentioned, U.S. Customs and Border Protection's (CBP) departure data primarily comes from passenger manifests for international flights, provided by the airline carriers. In some cases in FY 2014, it was apparent that there were errors in these manifests that contributed to larger errors in the FY 2014 Entry/Exit Overstay Report. Air carriers KLM (Royal Dutch Airlines) and Emirates had disproportionately high instances of passengers listed as "not on board" departing flights, despite the passengers having checked in for the flight.

Although CBP believes that a majority of these passengers were in fact aboard the flights, it should be noted that CBP cannot confirm this with absolute certainty as there is no record of the passengers' travel in the final departure manifest. CBP receives data from the carriers at multiple points in the arrival and departure process to best ensure data completeness. Since carriers provide manifest information well before a traveler actually boards the aircraft, CBP must rely on the carriers to identify which passengers boarded the aircraft and which did not at the time of the actual departure.

The Department concluded that these errors could erroneously identify certain VWP countries as having significant overstay rates, which could impact their ability to remain in the program. The FY 2015 data, which are now available, confirmed that these data errors have been corrected.

Because of the significant data errors for FY 2014, none of the overstay percentages for FY 2014 will be used to make any decisions as to whether any country will remain in the VWP.

Table 1

FY 2014 Overstay rates for nonimmigrant visitors admitted to the United States for business or pleasure (WB/WT/B-1/B-2) via air and sea POEs for VWP Countries

Country of Citizenship	Expected Departures	Out-of-Country Overstays	Suspected In-Country Overstays	Total Overstays	Overstay Rate	Suspected In-Country Overstay Rate
Andorra	1,215	1	5	6	0.49%	0.41%
Australia	1,273,201	907	4,721	5,628	0.44%	0.37%
Austria	213,380	124	1,681	1,805	0.85%	0.79%
Belgium	291,453	182	3,540	3,722	1.28%	1.21%
Brunei	1,317	-	20	20	1.52%	1.52%
Chile	241,828	235	3,673	3,908	1.62%	1.52%
Czech Republic	94,274	202	1,696	1,898	2.01%	1.80%
Denmark	303,053	171	5,352	5,523	1.82%	1.77%
Estonia	20,700	52	354	406	1.96%	1.71%
Finland	153,091	94	1,355	1,449	0.95%	0.89%
France	1,782,939	1,614	26,864	28,478	1.60%	1.51%
Germany	2,049,501	1,329	15,992	17,321	0.85%	0.78%
Greece	70,071	427	1,416	1,843	2.63%	2.02%
Hungary	71,335	376	2,320	2,696	3.78%	3.25%
Iceland	51,415	30	120	150	0.29%	0.23%
Ireland	448,556	352	1,940	2,292	0.51%	0.43%
Italy	1,166,428	1,360	31,164	32,524	2.79%	2.67%
Japan	3,069,506	414	6,149	6,563	0.21%	0.20%
Korea, South	1,023,581	1,404	9,729	11,133	1.09%	0.95%
Latvia	17,473	100	316	416	2.38%	1.81%
Liechtenstein	2,024	2	12	14	0.69%	0.59%
Lithuania	24,775	93	468	561	2.26%	1.89%
Luxembourg	14,396	3	264	267	1.85%	1.83%
Malta	5,786	11	58	69	1.19%	1.00%
Monaco	1,018	-	30	30	2.95%	2.95%
Netherlands	702,670	489	30,596	31,085	4.42%	4.35%
New Zealand	278,394	255	1,074	1,329	0.48%	0.39%
Norway	304,916	184	4,473	4,657	1.53%	1.47%
Portugal	164,499	525	3,383	3,908	2.38%	2.06%
San Marino	761	-	48	48	6.31%	6.31%
Singapore	127,267	102	540	642	0.50%	0.42%
Slovakia	41,645	115	724	839	2.01%	1.74%
Slovenia	21,122	33	255	288	1.36%	1.21%
Spain	867,187	1,734	11,969	13,703	1.58%	1.38%
Sweden	552,708	374	5,700	6,074	1.10%	1.03%
Switzerland	437,076	273	3,319	3,592	0.82%	0.76%

Taiwan	331,503	567	1,639	2,206	0.67%	0.49%
United Kingdom	4,216,065	2,636	17,914	20,550	0.49%	0.42%
TOTAL	**20,438,129**	**16,770**	**200,873**	**217,643**	**1.06%**	**0.98%**

Table 2
FY 2014 Overstay rates for nonimmigrants with B-1/B-2 visas admitted to the United States for business or pleasure via air and sea POEs for non-VWP Countries

Country Of Citizenship	Expected Departures	Out-of-Country Overstays	Suspected In-Country Overstays	Total Overstays	Overstay Rate	Suspected In-Country Overstays
Afghanistan	1,374	7	146	153	11.14%	10.63%
Albania	5,695	23	200	223	3.92%	3.51%
Algeria	7,640	25	149	174	2.28%	1.95%
Angola	9,967	29	247	276	2.77%	2.48%
Antigua and Barbuda	13,494	25	283	308	2.28%	2.10%
Argentina	720,391	193	9,214	9,407	1.31%	1.28%
Armenia	5,488	18	153	171	3.12%	2.79%
Azerbaijan	4,876	12	113	125	2.56%	2.32%
Bahamas, The	211,681	221	1,151	1,372	0.65%	0.54%
Bahrain	6,197	15	66	81	1.31%	1.07%
Bangladesh	23,000	69	1,726	1,795	7.80%	7.50%
Barbados	52,949	35	252	287	0.54%	0.48%
Belarus	10,968	19	166	185	1.69%	1.51%
Belize	22,507	49	421	470	2.09%	1.87%
Benin	1,829	4	102	106	5.80%	5.58%
Bhutan	281	2	55	57	20.29%	19.57%
Bolivia	46,025	62	817	879	1.91%	1.78%
Bosnia and Herzegovina	5,807	22	96	118	2.03%	1.65%
Botswana	1,507	2	25	27	1.79%	1.66%
Brazil	2,129,716	1,226	27,563	28,789	1.35%	1.29%
Bulgaria	24,629	79	415	494	2.01%	1.69%
Burkina Faso	2,643	17	258	275	10.41%	9.76%
Burma	2,946	9	55	64	2.17%	1.87%
Burundi	816	2	105	107	13.11%	12.87%
Cabo Verde	3,633	7	140	147	4.05%	3.85%
Cambodia	3,246	7	61	68	2.10%	1.88%
Cameroon	6,538	32	342	374	5.72%	5.23%
Central African Republic	177	1	13	14	7.91%	7.34%
Chad	499	1	45	46	9.22%	9.02%

Table 2

FY 2014 Overstay rates for nonimmigrants with B-1/B-2 visas admitted to the United States for business or pleasure via air and sea POEs for non-VWP Countries

Country Of Citizenship	Expected Departures	Out-of-Country Overstays	Suspected In-Country Overstays	Total Overstays	Overstay Rate	Suspected In-Country Overstays
China	1,436,742	2,214	15,792	18,006	1.25%	1.10%
Colombia	809,836	751	12,810	13,561	1.68%	1.58%
Comoros	88	-	-	0	0.00%	0.00%
Congo (Brazzaville)	1,106	7	53	60	5.43%	4.79%
Congo (Kinshasa)	3,975	29	269	298	7.50%	6.77%
Costa Rica	200,780	155	1,716	1,871	0.93%	0.85%
Croatia	18,600	37	163	200	1.08%	0.88%
Cuba	34,978	357	1,707	2,064	5.90%	4.88%
Cyprus	7,465	23	152	175	2.34%	2.04%
Côte d'Ivoire	4,938	20	169	189	3.83%	3.42%
Djibouti	206	1	56	57	27.67%	27.18%
Dominica	7,096	11	236	247	3.48%	3.33%
Dominican Republic	254,043	284	5,319	5,603	2.21%	2.09%
Ecuador	275,532	198	3,409	3,607	1.31%	1.24%
Egypt	70,690	264	1,715	1,979	2.80%	2.43%
El Salvador	111,752	121	1,743	1,864	1.67%	1.56%
Equatorial Guinea	1,001	11	42	53	5.30%	4.20%
Eritrea	1,528	71	211	282	18.46%	13.81%
Ethiopia	13,122	115	644	759	5.78%	4.91%
Fiji	6,795	20	133	153	2.25%	1.96%
Gabon	1,776	8	49	57	3.21%	2.76%
Gambia, The	2,005	17	223	240	11.97%	11.12%
Georgia	4,666	11	420	431	9.24%	9.00%
Ghana	21,719	97	887	984	4.53%	4.08%
Grenada	8,782	37	216	253	2.88%	2.46%
Guatemala	215,219	263	4,756	5,019	2.33%	2.21%
Guinea	1,607	12	116	128	7.97%	7.22%
Guinea-Bissau	117	1	8	9	7.69%	6.84%
Guyana	31,977	47	532	579	1.81%	1.66%
Haiti	101,151	521	2,270	2,791	2.76%	2.24%
Holy See	18	-	-	0	0.00%	0.00%
Honduras	148,665	169	3,376	3,545	2.39%	2.27%
India	766,936	1,254	10,399	11,653	1.52%	1.36%
Indonesia	79,171	89	888	977	1.23%	1.12%

Table 2

FY 2014 Overstay rates for nonimmigrants with B-1/B-2 visas admitted to the United States for business or pleasure via air and sea POEs for non-VWP Countries

Country Of Citizenship	Expected Departures	Out-of-Country Overstays	Suspected In-Country Overstays	Total Overstays	Overstay Rate	Suspected In-Country Overstays
Iran	16,429	85	441	526	3.20%	2.68%
Iraq	9,855	91	602	693	7.03%	6.11%
Israel	322,281	362	2,371	2,733	0.85%	0.74%
Jamaica	197,858	249	4,155	4,404	2.23%	2.10%
Jordan	26,022	117	912	1,029	3.95%	3.50%
Kazakhstan	15,070	36	628	664	4.41%	4.17%
Kenya	15,225	82	483	565	3.71%	3.17%
Kiribati	141	-	-	0	0.00%	0.00%
Korea, North	37	-	-	0	0.00%	0.00%
Kuwait	36,826	208	958	1,166	3.17%	2.60%
Kyrgyzstan	2,891	27	548	575	19.89%	18.96%
Laos	2,119	45	509	554	26.14%	24.02%
Lebanon	34,317	90	918	1,008	2.94%	2.68%
Lesotho	289	-	8	8	2.77%	2.77%
Liberia	3,420	67	296	363	10.61%	8.65%
Libya	1,368	6	76	82	5.99%	5.56%
Macedonia	5,328	18	216	234	4.39%	4.05%
Madagascar	694	-	14	14	2.02%	2.02%
Malawi	1,483	2	53	55	3.71%	3.57%
Malaysia	80,411	90	1,392	1,482	1.84%	1.73%
Maldives	193	-	5	5	2.59%	2.59%
Mali	2,972	12	212	224	7.54%	7.13%
Marshall Islands	80	4	2	6	7.50%	2.50%
Mauritania	1,038	4	105	109	10.50%	10.12%
Mauritius	2,633	3	28	31	1.18%	1.06%
Micronesia, Federated States of	29	2	1	3	10.35%	3.45%
Moldova	6,703	31	292	323	4.82%	4.36%
Mongolia	9,077	35	107	142	1.56%	1.18%
Montenegro	3,214	8	76	84	2.61%	2.36%
Morocco	22,700	78	473	551	2.43%	2.08%
Mozambique	1,637	5	24	29	1.77%	1.47%
Namibia	1,510	2	27	29	1.92%	1.79%
Nauru	13	-	-	0	0.00%	0.00%
Nepal	11,895	39	414	453	3.81%	3.48%
Nicaragua	53,654	80	830	910	1.70%	1.55%
Niger	765	5	28	33	4.31%	3.66%

Table 2

FY 2014 Overstay rates for nonimmigrants with B-1/B-2 visas admitted to the United States for business or pleasure via air and sea POEs for non-VWP Countries

Country Of Citizenship	Expected Departures	Out-of-Country Overstays	Suspected In-Country Overstays	Total Overstays	Overstay Rate	Suspected In-Country Overstays
Nigeria	150,307	510	4,079	4,589	3.05%	2.71%
Oman	4,120	18	60	78	1.89%	1.46%
Pakistan	55,551	141	1,232	1,373	2.47%	2.22%
Palau	37	-	2	2	5.41%	5.41%
Panama	138,963	109	658	767	0.55%	0.47%
Papua New Guinea	719	-	7	7	0.97%	0.97%
Paraguay	26,131	32	479	511	1.96%	1.83%
Peru	239,498	291	2,823	3,114	1.30%	1.18%
Philippines	197,513	467	2,978	3,445	1.74%	1.51%
Poland	152,845	228	2,327	2,555	1.67%	1.52%
Qatar	11,926	91	155	246	2.06%	1.30%
Romania	57,059	166	1,343	1,509	2.65%	2.35%
Russia	325,039	268	2,395	2,663	0.82%	0.74%
Rwanda	2,105	8	99	107	5.08%	4.70%
Saint Kitts and Nevis	10,667	19	224	243	2.28%	2.10%
Saint Lucia	13,429	25	319	344	2.56%	2.38%
Saint Vincent and the Grenadines	8,602	26	320	346	4.02%	3.72%
Samoa	1,685	13	76	89	5.28%	4.51%
Sao Tome and Principe	54	-	-	0	0.00%	0.00%
Saudi Arabia	110,985	401	1,170	1,571	1.42%	1.05%
Senegal	7,927	36	293	329	4.15%	3.70%
Serbia	17,422	33	295	328	1.88%	1.69%
Seychelles	276	1	1	2	0.73%	0.36%
Sierra Leone	2,509	19	118	137	5.46%	4.70%
Solomon Islands	163	-	3	3	1.84%	1.84%
Somalia	100	2	3	5	5.00%	3.00%
South Africa	115,482	144	992	1,136	0.98%	0.86%
South Sudan	143	-	2	2	1.40%	1.40%
Sri Lanka	13,935	30	458	488	3.50%	3.29%
Sudan	2,685	14	214	228	8.49%	7.97%
Suriname	10,872	5	52	57	0.52%	0.48%
Swaziland	598	1	7	8	1.34%	1.17%
Syria	13,297	144	720	864	6.50%	5.41%

Table 2

FY 2014 Overstay rates for nonimmigrants with B-1/B-2 visas admitted to the United States for business or pleasure via air and sea POEs for non-VWP Countries

Country Of Citizenship	Expected Departures	Out-of-Country Overstays	Suspected In-Country Overstays	Total Overstays	Overstay Rate	Suspected In-Country Overstays
Tajikistan	849	7	29	36	4.24%	3.42%
Tanzania	4,556	29	104	133	2.92%	2.28%
Thailand	78,810	105	1,278	1,383	1.76%	1.62%
Timor-Leste	26	-	-	0	0.00%	0.00%
Togo	1,455	8	93	101	6.94%	6.39%
Tonga	1,880	5	74	79	4.20%	3.94%
Trinidad and Tobago	146,970	94	694	788	0.54%	0.47%
Tunisia	8,062	15	167	182	2.26%	2.07%
Turkey	152,041	185	2,802	2,987	1.97%	1.84%
Turkmenistan	913	3	47	50	5.48%	5.15%
Tuvalu	47	1	-	1	2.13%	0.00%
Uganda	6,467	26	221	247	3.82%	3.42%
Ukraine	63,231	146	1,450	1,596	2.52%	2.29%
United Arab Emirates	23,470	178	386	564	2.40%	1.64%
Uruguay	66,244	51	1,114	1,165	1.76%	1.68%
Uzbekistan	7,758	49	534	583	7.52%	6.88%
Vanuatu	88	-	2	2	2.27%	2.27%
Venezuela	779,882	369	6,896	7,265	0.93%	0.88%
Vietnam	54,041	269	936	1,205	2.23%	1.73%
Yemen	2,493	13	160	173	6.94%	6.42%
Zambia	3,323	9	96	105	3.16%	2.89%
Zimbabwe	5,327	18	87	105	1.97%	1.63%
TOTAL	11,961,355	16,133	173,136	189,269	1.58%	1.45%

Table 3

FY 2014 Overstay rates for Canadian and Mexican nonimmigrants admitted to the United States for business or pleasure via air and sea POEs

Country of Citizenship	Expected Departures	Out-of-Country Overstays	Suspected In-Country Overstays	Total Overstays	Overstay Rate	Suspected In-Country Overstay Rate
Canada	7,721,124	7,710	82,493	90,203	1.17%	1.07%
Mexico	2,673,330	2,912	34,315	37,227	1.39%	1.28%
TOTAL	**10,394,454**	**10,622**	**116,808**	**127,430**	**1.22%**	**1.12%**